PRAYER 101

Dear Dr. Gwen,
 May God always bless you abundantly.
 Quinita

QUINITA EDMONIA GOOD

PRAYER 101

HOW TO FORM A CONSISTENT PRAYER LIFE

SECOND EDITION

TATE PUBLISHING
AND ENTERPRISES, LLC

Prayer 101
Copyright © 2014 by Quinita Edmonia Good. All rights reserved.

No part of this publication may be reproduced, stored in a retrieval system or transmitted in any way by any means, electronic, mechanical, photocopy, recording or otherwise without the prior permission of the author except as provided by USA copyright law.

The opinions expressed by the author are not necessarily those of Tate Publishing, LLC.

Published by Tate Publishing & Enterprises, LLC
127 E. Trade Center Terrace | Mustang, Oklahoma 73064 USA
1.888.361.9473 | www.tatepublishing.com

Tate Publishing is committed to excellence in the publishing industry. The company reflects the philosophy established by the founders, based on Psalm 68:11,
"The Lord gave the word and great was the company of those who published it."

Book design copyright © 2014 by Tate Publishing, LLC. All rights reserved.
Cover design by Allen Jomoc
Interior design by Caypeeline Casas

Published in the United States of America

ISBN: 978-1-63185-130-8
1. Religion / Prayerbooks / Christian
2. Religion / Spirituality
14.04.04

I dedicate this book to my mother who always kept the family bible with our family legacy on the living room table when I was young. I'll always thank her for teaching me to pray the "Now I lay me down to sleep…" prayer, for through that prayer, I learned to turn many things over to God.

Acknowledgements

I would like to acknowledge the memory of my maternal grandmother Alberta Edmonia Nelson Moore for being the example I so sorely needed in my life. Her favorite words were "let's wait and see." Today, these words, for me, resonate the scripture, "be still know that I am God." I will always remember her with gratitude and respect for being the type of woman I aspire to become.

My Testimony

Ever since I can remember, I was a daddy's girl. My favorite places were on his lap, across his breast, over his shoulders, and in between his knees. His very voice was my command to attention. Yes, I loved him beyond measure. In a sense, he was my god. He was the pleasure I never wanted to part with.

All of this fell apart when he and my mother split and he moved away to a distant city. I was left alone with my mother and grandparents. I remember a lot of time going by when all I did was cry for him to come home. I worshipped him and felt abandoned when he left. But, his leaving did not deter my love for him. I was forever his, no matter what he did or said or anyone else for that matter. After all, he was my daddy.

Growing up, my father was, well, missing in action. Besides occasional phone calls and letters, or visits on some holidays like Christmas, or when we went to Chicago or Peoria, Illinois, where he lived, I did not see or hear from him. For the most part, we did not have contact. It wasn't until my adult years that I realized the impact this separation had on me.

As a teenager, I began to experiment with marijuana and other drugs. I became sexually promiscuous and began to look for my daddy in other men. Oddly enough, I could never sustain a relationship for more than a few weeks or months, always sabotaging the closeness for the separation I felt was inevitable.

Although I longed for a satisfying, committed relationship as I got older, I seemed unable to maintain them. It was a vicious cycle: meet a nice man, put my best foot forward with him, find his weaknesses, become dissatisfied, and sabotage the relationship. I always felt disagreements were final. It never occurred to me that I could work things out with another human being.

In my early twenties, I continued to experiment with drugs—marijuana for the high, mescaline for the energy, and cocaine for the escape. My lifestyle was such that I began to draw to me men who could only use me for sexual purposes, or so I thought. I began to see my body as a viable tool for getting men to do what I wanted. I looked to new age and pornographic books and movies to teach me how to hone this talent I then felt was innate in me. But my love for my daddy never diminished. Somewhere, I longed to meet a man like him—powerful, commanding, and able to teach.

One night, I met my son's father at a party. He seemed genuinely interested in one of my girlfriends. But this only fueled my motivation toward getting him to like me. Before the party was over, we exchanged phone numbers and thereafter began a relationship, which was mostly sexual.

Although he expressed to me that he didn't want any more children—he had a daughter and felt trapped by the experience—I became pregnant three months into the relationship. As many girls around me were getting pregnant, I was very ecstatic about the possibilities of becoming a mother. However, my new man was devastated. He quickly cut ties with me and went his separate way. This proved to be a harrowing experience for both of us—he, not wanting children, becoming a father again; and me dreaming of a family of my own only with him set on not being with us.

I was so taken aback that I considered having an abortion, when one night I was laying on the couch with my eyes closed and envisioned a baby's face. God was trying to show me the child I would have. His face was beautiful, almost angelic. And his countenance was peaceful and full of joy. It was then I decided that I could not abort this child.

On April 2nd, 1980, at 9:50am in the morning, my son was born naturally, after 52 hours of labor. He looked exactly like the baby in the vision I had before.

My dad was not there to see this beautiful child come into the world. Although my mother, maternal grandmother, my son's father and my coach were there, I really wanted my dad to be there. Because he wasn't, I felt especially alone and deprived.

My son's father came back into our lives for a short-lived period, but quickly made another exit—this time for good.

The pressures of being a single mom were overwhelming. As the years passed, I secretly longed for a man who would be my husband and a father to my son. I tried to no avail to make this happen, often resorting to my old ways of trying to capture a man through sex to make it happen.

Like before, my criteria for choosing a mate were that he would be powerful, commanding, and able to teach like my dad. One day, I met such a man. He was tall, dark, handsome, and met all of the criteria I sought.

In my eyes, this man was like a god. Everything he did or said was scripture for me. Before I knew it, I was doing things contrary to what I had been raised to do.

I remember my mother telling me during this time that I was making myself too available to him. But I did not listen. As I did my dad, I began to worship this man and, in my eyes, he could do no wrong.

True to my cycle, this man, too, left out of my life. I was devastated. On February 14, 1990 (Valentine's Day), I experienced a break with reality. I began to see and hear evil things and was diagnosed in the hospital as being schizophrenic.

The doctors quickly put me on antipsychotic medicines and sent me home to deal with problems I had no experience dealing with. This turning point in my life proved to be very valuable, but I did not see it at first.

Not being used to taking medicine, I threw away all of my pills and decided I would no longer need them. Well, needless to say, the evil visions and voices came back. Not being able to deal with such, I thought that I would take my life.

One day, my brother whom I lived with was at work and my son was in school. I was home alone. I went into the kitchen and got a steak knife and took it into the living room where I laid down on the floor. Because I believed that it is a sin to take one's life, I asked God's forgiveness, then drove the knife through my chest. Blood was all over my clothes, but I didn't feel any different than before. I got on the phone and called a friend to ask if she could pick my son up from after-school care and keep him until my brother got there. She refused and rushed me off the phone. I did not tell her what I had done. I went into the bathroom and put a bandage over my wound and changed clothes. Then, I went to the couch and laid down to sleep, so sure I would die in my sleep.

A couple of hours later, I woke up. My wound had only bled a little bit more and, still, I felt no different. I began to blame myself for not being able to even kill myself right. Little did I know, the Lord was preserving me. Yet, in my eyes, there was nothing that I could do right. I laid on the couch in self-pity.

I must have laid there for over an hour when the telephone rang. It was my son's after-school program. Someone needed to pick him up. I quickly put another bandage on my wound and changed my top and went out the door to pick my son up.

In this situation, one should always seek help. But I was beyond that point of personal intervention. I was not thinking clearly.

When I got my son home from the program, I acted as if nothing happened. I got him home and put dinner on so my brother and he could have something hot for that cold Spring day.

When my brother got home from work, he must have noticed that I was disillusioned and he told me he was going to take me to the hospital. Once in the emergency room stall, I showed my brother my wound and asked him not to tell anyone. But because he was level-headed and cared for me, he told the doctor. Before I knew it, I was in the ICU unit where there were tubes and wires coming and going out of me everywhere. I think I was there about a week when they told me the knife had come within an inch of my heart and that they would be sending me to the psyche ward from there.

Two weeks in the psyche ward and I was sent home with more medicine and the feeling that I was a hopeless and embarrassing case. Most of my friends alienated themselves from me. I felt that I couldn't get anything right and that now no man would want me.

For 22 years from that day, I spent most of my time in the bed, sleeping and worrying. I disconnected myself from life. I neglected my duties as a mother and often sought to placate my son when he really needed me.

Somewhere along the line, though, I began to pray to Jehovah and then, also to Jesus and the Holy Spirit. First, I began to recite rote prayers, then—out of my frustration—I began to talk to God as I would a friend.

Every time I would be vexed by my situation, I would pray. Sometimes, I would call someone to pray for me over the telephone. My favorite prayer times were when a longtime friend of mine would pray for me while I was listening. She is a great prayer warrior and sometimes would prophetically call out what was going on with me. This was especially comforting, because I felt God was using her to let me know that He was listening. I also tried attending many different churches until I gave up on them as well.

In May of 2009, I believe God redeemed me. I rededicated my life to Jesus Christ and returned to Trinity Temple Church of God in Christ in Montclair, NJ, as my home church. I have to tell you that since that time, I have been encouraged to read my bible, pray, and meditate on God's word. I was also taught to rely on the Holy Spirit before I make decisions and to actually prophesy good things over my life, always looking to God's Word in the Bible for direction and motivation.

Yet, for someone undergoing psychiatric treatment, it is important to take the medicine as prescribed and engage in therapy. This, coupled with my belief in God has sustained me thus far.

I do have to tell you that I am no longer diagnosed as schizophrenic. I continue to keep appointments with my psychiatrist and therapist and now am in remission. I have re-engaged a relationship with God and with my earthly father and have made peace with both of them.

My son is well-adjusted and has a beautiful daughter, and my brother continues to be a support to both of us.

Through everything, I have found that prayer and supplication to the Lord Jesus Christ has been my earthly salvation. I no longer fear separation and loneliness, because I realize that God has always been there for me, even when human beings could not be.

Today, I do not lead a perfect white-picket-fence life, but my life is manageable and I have learned to stand with an attitude of gratitude in everything I experience. Having a consistent prayer life has truly been my saving grace.

My goal for this book is that my testimony and the prayers herein will reassure you that life really is worth living, that no weapon formed against you can prosper, and that there is a God who truly cares for you.

Quinita Edmonia Good

Introduction

Have you or someone you know spent time trying to pray and the words didn't come as easily as you thought? Are you a new Christian, wanting to speak to God from your heart and you're not sure what to say or how to say it? Have you been a believer for some time and, right through here, your heart is heavy with concern and you can't seem to communicate what you feel to God?

This book is meant for those who struggle in prayer looking for words, wrestling with thoughts and feelings, and wondering if God hears.

It is important to note that the Holy Spirit reads your heart even before you pray. God, the Father, searches our hearts, and Jesus the Christ offers salvation and healing for all who come to Him. It doesn't matter if you are just beginning to pray or have prayed for many years, God embraces all. The Bible says that Jesus came to "all men." You don't have to worry about sending God beautiful words and long descriptions. The Bible says that God knows our need even before we ask. Although we sometimes struggle in prayer, He wants us to know that He is comfort in a storm, a beacon of light in the darkness, and that He is Love Himself.

People have given God many names. Among them is the name Jehovah-Jireh, meaning God the Provider. To access God as our Jehovah-Jireh, we would need to relinquish the outcomes we come up with and put our total trust in Him; trusting that He has our best interests at heart. This isn't easy for most folks, but it is attainable when we realize—as the Bible tells us—God is Spirit and God is Love.

Pure love is unconditional. It does not discriminate and it heals all brokenness. This book is not meant to take the place of the Bible or any other prayer or devotional book. It was written to support you in your time of need. It may not be the answer to your prayers, but it can facilitate the beginning of a consistent prayer life.

I must mention here that prayer alone does not work. You must believe that God exists and that He rewards those who diligently seek Him. In other words, you must have faith that there is a God and that He cares for you.

I know that it's difficult to believe when you have no relationship with the Lord. That is why reading your Bible is essential. Therein, you will find many accounts of God's relationship with people who believed in Him and how he answered their prayers. There is a great scripture in the Bible that says God's Word will not return unto Him void (Isaiah 55:11). The Bible is filled with God's covenants and promises. If you will try Him, He will not disappoint you.

Sometimes, God answers our prayers right away. At other times, He tells us to wait. And, sometimes God will tell us "no." Remember that God knows best and that all of His answers are in our best interests. The Bible says that His ways are higher than our ways and His thoughts are higher than ours.

If you are not sure what God is telling you, wait for clarity in His answer. If you can help it, you should never make a decision when you are confused or when your emotions are wrenching. God's Word tells us, "Be still and know that I Am God." His answers can come in many ways, including through a song, a word of encouragement, or through searching the Scriptures. God's answers will always line-up with His Word in the Bible.

The following prayers can be read, recited, or used in portions. They are meant to comfort you and give you a way to communicate when you're not sure how to.

When you know God's answer, you will feel a peace about it. If need be, you will act with courage and confidence. Remember, Jesus said that when we experience bad things to be of good cheer for He has already overcome the world.

Love,
Quinita

A Single Woman's Song

Dear God,

I love the way you made me. Your Word says that I am fearfully and wonderfully made; that I am your child, your daughter, a co-heir with Jesus Christ. Because you are the King of Kings, that makes me royalty!

I thank you for being my Father, full of loving kindness, long-suffering, and mercy. No matter what I've said or done, You've said that You would never leave me nor forsake me. For this I'm truly grateful.

Now, Lord, I ask that You continue to be my covering; an ever-present protection of my womanhood; providing for my needs and applying your healing balm where I am deficient.

I ask that you give me Your favor in all things and with all men. I promise to continue to draw near to you and ask that you bless my singleness in heart with right-relationships, joy in my heart, peace in my mind and strength in my spirit. In Jesus' name I pray. Amen.

Prayer for Children

Dear Lord,

I pray that you bless my little angels; the children that you have lent to me this day of my parenthood. Give me what I need to be the best parent I can be to them. Your Word says that children are a heritage of the Lord and that the fruit of my womb and seed of my loins are my reward. Thank you for entrusting these young lives to me. Make me able to accept my responsibility and care for them in the way I should.

Lord, Your Word says that great shall be the peace of my children. Send your ministering and protecting angels to encamp round about them, lest they dash their feet against a stone. Yea, put a hedge of protection around them and surround them with your love and mercy.

I will teach my children of You and Your ways. I call all things that are not as though they were. As for me and my house, we shall serve the Lord with all our hearts and minds.

My grown children, too, shall serve You, O Lord. Even if my children have entered adulthood, I will continue to pray for them and seek You on their behalf. Bless them in their coming out and going in. Make them the head and not the tail. Help them make right decisions and align themselves with people who have good intentions.

Give them favor in all things and with all men. Dear God, be a lamp unto their feet and a light unto their paths. Make them a beacon of light for our families and our communities, even our nations.

Give them a spirit of excellence in their studies and cause them to learn effectively and efficiently. Heal them in their bodies when they are sick and bless them in mind and spirit as well.

Teach them Your ways, commandments, and statutes. Cause them to be great men and women of God. In Jesus' precious name I pray. Amen.

Prayer for Couples

Dear God,

Thank You for entrusting to me the love and life of my beloved. Help me to act responsibly toward them and to uplift them whenever and wherever I can. Lord, Your Word says that I should drink waters out of my own cistern, and running waters out of my own well. Help me to be willing to delve into the depths of this marriage with the virtues of patience, love, hope, and faith.

Father, help me to see now the beauty in my spouse that I saw when I first met them. Help me not to lose sight of their vision and potential. Help me to quickly mend disagreements with love and understanding. Help me to follow their lead when needed and help me to encourage and uplift them always.

Lord, I pray that you bless our family and help us to understand and remember the mystery of two becoming one. In Jesus' name I pray. Amen

Prayer for Healing

Elohim, El Shadai, Jehovah-Jireh. You are my Jehovah-Rophe (God our Healer). You, my God, are the God of the Universe. My flesh was formed by Your holy hands, my spirit by the majesty of Your breath. I worship You today and always. Holy, Holy, Holy, Lord God Almighty, I praise you today and forevermore! As it says in Your Word, "I am fearfully and wonderfully made."

Dear God, please cleanse my mind and my heart. Make me a vessel unto your honor that I may approach the Throne of Grace cleansed of my iniquity, dis-ease, and sins.

Lord, I thank you for my being able to think clearly. Dear God I thank you for all those abilities that you have given me that are working properly, causing me to sense clearly. I thank and honor You for my life and the ability to approach You with this petition. Dear God, I ask for the healing of _____. I know that Your Word says that "by His (Jesus) stripes we are healed." Lord, You also said that your Word will not return unto You void. Touch every ailing part of _____ and resurrect _____ into perfect heath.

From this moment further, I choose to walk in faith that You, Oh God, will accomplish Your Will on Earth as it is in Heaven and that all of us will be restored according to your Will.

I surrender to you, Oh Lord, all my wants and desires, except those that You bring back to me through divine revelation. I release all control to You, and I watch and wait for your move in my life and in the life of _____.
By your stripes, healing takes place. In Jesus' precious name I pray. Thank you, God. Amen.

Prayer for Right Relationship

God of my heart, Captain of my soul, I praise Your Holy Name. You alone are holy. You alone are God. There is none above You. There is none greater than You. I stand in worship of You and Your holy ways. For You said that "Your thoughts are higher than my thoughts and Your ways higher than mine."

Lord cleanse every part of me that is not pleasing unto You. Prepare me to be a sanctuary for Your Holy Spirit. Look within me, Oh Lord, and erase that which is not pleasing unto your Holy Eyes. In this moment of repentance, Oh Lord, I offer up a sweet savory fragrance that is befitting the King that I serve.

Thank You, Lord, for all that you have done for me and all that You are yet doing. I thank You that I have my right mind. I thank You for all the blessings You have poured into my life. I thank You for family and friends. I thank You, because You know all my needs and as I am yet praying, you have answered my prayer. I thank You most, Dear Lord, for my relationship with You.

Dear God, I open my heart so that You may pour into my life right relationships with others; relationships that are mutually nurturing, conducted as safe havens, bearing trust and growth. Likewise, my Lord, I lovingly release all those who cannot walk with me. You choose for me. Because you said "do not be yoked with unbelievers." Today, is the first day of a long and satisfying life with You.

In faith, I thank you for allowing me to experience all the good that relationships bring and the lessons that relationships teach. I choose to learn and grow through those whom You have chosen to cross my path and those You choose to walk with me, as well as through Your Holy Word.

Today, I surrender to Your Holy Will and I praise You, Dear Lord, with all my heart. In Jesus' precious Name I pray. Amen.

Prayer for Decision-Making

Praise be to the Father, the Son, and the Holy Spirit. Today, I take this moment to minister unto my Lord. Humbly, I place my God before everyone and anything that I have previously held in importance. You, Oh God, are omniscient. You, Oh God, are my peaceful habitation. When I think of You, I know that You are the Source of all my good. As the old ones say, You are my Doctor, my Lawyer, my Mother, and my Father. Without You, I am but dust. Yet with You, I am blessed going out and blessed coming in. With You, oh God, I am blessed.

As Your Word says, I am "…fearfully and wonderfully made." I love myself and I trust all the wonderful abilities you have given me. Today, I will remember to walk in Your Love and live as a precious vessel unto you.

Thank you, God for the very breath in my body and the fact that I still dwell on this Earth. Yes, Lord, I thank you for my very life.

Today, I find myself at the crossroads once again. I have decisions to make and I am unsure. Yet, Your Word says that "confusion is not of God." Therefore, my Lord, I humbly ask Your assistance in making the right decision. I promise that I will not move until I hear from You. Yes, I will rest in You, because I know that the battle is not mine, but the Lord's. I thank you in advance for Your mighty move in my life.

My God, I know that You have delivered me many times before, and I stand on these experiences as evidence of Your Love for me, as well as the fact that You *can* do it again.

I have also seen You deliver many family members and friends who called upon You in moments of trouble. I know that what You did for them, You can also do for me because Your Word says that You "are not a respecter of persons."

So, today, in Jesus' name I banish all doubt and confusion, and I experience my highest good through You.

I pray that the right decisions that You will help me make will come clearly. I surrender all my fears and doubts unto you, Oh Lord, and I ask that You continue to look favorably on me as Your child, and I will "be still and know that You are God."

In Jesus' Mighty Name I pray. Amen.

Prayer for the Unemployed

Father God, I stand in the need of a vocation that will utilize my talents, dreams, and aspirations. Help me to get in touch with what it is you want out of me on this Earth. Guide me in my search for valuable work and service.

During this time of unemployment, help me to use my time wisely and ready myself for Your vision for me. Your Word says that I should not lean unto my own understanding, but in all my ways acknowledge You and You will direct my paths. Direct me, O Lord, in the way that I should go.

Father, help me to not become discouraged, but in all things to pray and present my challenges to You. Father, Your Word says that I should be strong and let not my hands be weak: for my work shall be rewarded.

Give me favor in Your sight and in the sight of man. Bless everything I put my hands to, and help me to not forget that all control is in Your hands. Help me to know that as I am looking for work, that all my needs will be supplied according to Your riches and Glory, through Christ Jesus. Amen.

Prayer for Peace of Mind

I'm spinning, God. There are so many thoughts in my mind interrupting my sleep and causing me despair. I realize that somewhere along my journey, I have allowed other things and people to take precedence over You.

Today, I lovingly release all that have attached themselves to me, begging me of things that only You can give. Today, I realize that I have also been looking for these things in others and that this is the reason I feel so desperate and depleted. Deep within, I know that no one can give me what You can.

Today, I thank You for sparing my life and allowing me to realize that You are the Source of my sustenance, my joy.

I surrender all control to You, and I humbly invite You into my Life once more. In Jesus' precious name I pray. Amen.

Prayer for Self-Realization

Here am I, God, on bended knee. I am made in Your magnificent image, yet I don't feel like the person you made me to be. I am angry and I am in pain. I smell like things of the world. Contrary to your Word, I feel so unworthy.

Help me, Lord, to accept myself as I am. I am your child. Your Word says that I am fearfully and wonderfully made. Thank You for You God, because with You I am reminded of the beauty You gave me. I am Your precious child. I stand on your Word that says "greater is He that is in me than he that is in the world."

Lover of all lovers, I stand in Your truth, which says that I am the head and not the tail, above and not beneath, more than a conqueror, a true child of Yours. I am humbled. Thank You for reminding me. I love You, too. I am no longer angry, because You are Love that shows me the difference between who I was yesterday and who I am right now. In Jesus Christ, I am a new creature. I thank You, Lord! In Jesus' name I pray. Amen.

Prayer for Forgiveness

The Gospel of Mark 11:25 says that we should stand when forgiving others who have wronged us.

Father God, I stand guilty of holding ought against my friend. No matter what we say, we cannot see eye to eye. Your Word says that if I have something against someone, that I should first go to them and resolve it.

Now Lord, I know I must turn to You and ask forgiveness for the way I've behaved. Because of You, I know that the only person I can make a change in is me. So I look to You Father and I ask that You soften my heart toward my friend and myself. Teach me, Oh Lord, to see them as You see them. And, Lord, teach me to walk and behave as You would have me to do. With all my heart, I forgive both myself and my friend and from this day forward I will remember how much You love me.

Lord, You love me so much that You sent Your Son to erase my sins and reconcile me back unto You. I realize, Lord, that reconciliation is a daily walk and that I must commit each day to You.

Now, I lovingly and freely release my friend and our problems unto You. For the Bible says that Your "yoke is easy and (Your) burden is light," and within Your bosom there is love.

In Jesus' precious name I pray. Amen.

Prayer for Family

Precious Lord, You are the originator of the family. After all needs were met, you blew the breath of life into man and woman and created living and breathing human beings. Your Word says that it was not good for man to be alone, so you created woman to be a help-meet. Whether I walk with a spouse, extended family, or alone, I know that You consider me Your precious child. In fact, because you are King, I am royalty.

With this in mind, dear Father, please help me and my family to walk in agreement with You. Help us to remember that prayer is a family affair and that we can accomplish so much more with You on our side.

Help us to take our concerns and needs to You and listen intently so that we may be in tune with Your guidance. Help us also to remember to include our children in prayer and bring them up—as the Bible says—"in the way they should go and they will not depart from it."

Even if my family is torn in and of itself, I pray that You mend the breach between us. Give us understanding of one another and help us to act with wisdom.

God, You are our rearward—with You, we cannot go wrong because You have our backs. Let me not try to change my family members, but allow me to look within to see where I can change myself.

Thank you for this precious circle called family. I now place my loved ones and myself in Your precious care. In Jesus' loving name I pray. Amen.

Prayer of Gratitude

Today, I cast my cares out to sea. Every concern, problem, and/or worry is now insignificant compared to the power and beauty of our God. I am free.

Freedom means that I have options and choices. Today, I choose to be grateful for who I am; for who God made me to be. It does not matter that I may not have a car, a home, a plethora of friends, or material creature comforts. I have life. God's Word says that He came to give us Life and Life more abundantly. As long as I have breath in my body, I will not only survive; I will thrive.

Dear God, Your Word says that I am the head and not the tail; above and not beneath. Your Word also says I shall lend and not borrow; and as a descendant of Abraham, my generations will be blessed. Thank You, God, that I am able to breathe, that I am able to see, feel, hear, and touch. Thank you God for loving me. Thank You God for the hedge of protection surrounding me. As for me and my house—whether it be many or one—we will serve the Lord!

With Your divine guidance, I will move beyond where I am into the place and space You want me to be. Today, I am willing and open to become the person you have destined me to be. Today, I am grateful that I have You for a friend because I know that You will stick closer than a brother.

Thank You, God, for loving me and giving me the vision and strength I need to press on. Today, I stand in an attitude of gratitude. In Jesus name. Amen.

Prayer for Loneliness

Lord, there are times when I feel all alone in this world. It seems as though I have nowhere to turn and no one to turn to. But You have said that You will never leave me nor forsake me, and I know Your Word will not return unto You void.

Lord, You have also said if You be for me, who can be against me. With Your army of angels on the way or already here, I am safe within your reach. In every situation, I am more than a conqueror!

Your Word says, "greater is He that is in (me) than he that is in the world."

Today, I may not find the human touch I desire, but I know beyond a shadow of a doubt that you are with me, guiding me, protecting me, keeping me, and sheltering me. In Your Presence, I am never alone.

God, I know that if I draw near to You, You will draw near to me. I know with all my heart that all I need to do is exercise my faith and Your promises will come alive in my life, because You said that if I seek truth and mercy, I will gain the favor of God and man. Oh Lord, how I need you!

I will not drown in self-pity or any kind of poverty. I will wait, I say I will wait on the Lord, and You will renew my strength. This battle is not mine, it belongs to God.

My family and I are free, and even if they are not with me now, the freedom that we enjoy in the Lord surpasses any separation or loneliness. In Jesus' precious name I pray. Amen!

Prayer for Grief

Dear God,

There's so much I don't understand about death and the afterlife. You said that, in order to be with you when we die, we need to accept Jesus as our Lord and Savior. I may not be sure that my loved one has done this, but I ask that You embrace their spirit.

I know that You can do all things. I know that, with You, all things are possible. I know that You can save anytime You get ready. I ask that You save my loved one and prepare a place for them in your heavenly kingdom.

Please give me the strength to go on, knowing that I will meet them one day in heaven. Help me to remember the beautiful things about them and release them to Your loving care.

I may not know much about death and the afterlife, but I do not that You are in control. Now I ask that You comfort me by Your Holy Spirit. Lead and guide me into all truth. Above all, dear Lord, ease my pain and help me to carry on.

In Jesus' name I pray. Amen.

During Times of Separation & Divorce

In this moment, I would like to share some things with you that have been tried and proven to be true. Initially, I would like to let you know that I have never been married, but I do know what the Lord says about marriage. I have been in love. I know what the loss of love feels like, and I know what it's like to try all you know how to what seems to be no avail. But because my experience has been somewhat limited and at times skewed, I want to approach this subject from what the Bible tells us about love and marriage.

First of all, see Proverbs 18:22, which says "Whoso findeth a wife findeth a good thing, and obtaineth favour of the Lord" (KJV). This principle clearly means that it is the man that pursues, not the woman. It also implies that if the man pursues and finds, he has found favor in the Lord's eyes. It does not give this directive to women. Therefore, it is not favorable for a woman to pursue a man.

Also see Ephesians 5:33. It tells us that a man must love his wife, and a wife must respect her husband. This does not mean that a woman shouldn't love her husband also. It's just that if a man loves his wife as he loves himself and the wife respects her husband, more harmony can exist between them, and the union, too, will be blessed.

Brothers and sisters, we have all made mistakes that have cost us dearly. We must ask God to forgive us our mistakes. Then we must forgive ourselves and our loves. You've done things your way; now try doing them God's way.

When it comes to divorce, Jesus says, "Haven't you read, he replied, that at the beginning the Creator made them male and female, and said, 'For this reason a man will leave his father and mother and be united to his wife, and the two will become one flesh'? So they are no longer two, but one. Therefore what God has joined together, let man not separate." (Mt 19:4-6–NIV).

Jesus later explains that Moses allowed divorce because our hearts were hard. There Jesus said, "I tell you that anyone who divorces his wife, except for marital unfaithfulness, and marries another woman commits adultery," (Mt 19:9—NIV).

Most bibles have a concordance in the back that gives scripture references on different topics. Try looking up marriage, wife, husband, love, divorce, reunion, and joy.

Heavenly Father, I pray that the person reading this will soften their hearts toward You and allow You to mold and shape them into the person you would have them be. I pray that they are open to your unfailing love and your unending faithfulness and that their love not be conditional for themselves or their beloveds, but that in their own weaknesses, You are Strong. In Jesus' precious name I pray, Amen.

Prayer for Salvation

Dear Jesus,

I realize that I cannot do this life thing alone. I confess my sins to You and ask that You forgive them. Please come into my life and be my Lord and Savior. Today, I give my life to You. In Your precious name I pray. Amen.

_____

Name

_____

Date

Prayer for Protection

Dear God,

I acknowledge that You are Strong and Mighty in Battle; that You are more powerful than anyone, any spirit, any illness, and anything. For the battle is not mine, but the Lord's.

Lord, Your Word says that you "did not give us the spirit of fear, but of love, power, and a sound mind." I believe Your Word! I rest in your protection.

Lord, it only seems that the enemy is prevailing against me, attacking me on every side. Yet, you said that I must "resist the devil and he will flee" from me. Grant me faith dear Lord, for "faith is the substance of things hoped for, the evidence of things unseen."

I ask that you put a hedge of protection around me and mine; that your ministering and protecting angels will encamp round about us. Your Word says that "a thousand will fall at (my) right hand and ten thousand at (my) left, but it shall not come nigh (me)" (KJV). I stand on your promises. "No weapon formed against me shall prosper, and every tongue that rises against me, I shall condemn. "As for me and my house, we will serve the Lord."

Because you have given me power, I stand strong in You and I bind the enemy on every front.

No hurt, harm or danger shall come near me and mine. In Jesus' precious name I declare! Amen.

Notes:

DATE PRAYER WAS MADE

NAME OF PERSON PRAYED FOR

DATE PRAYER WAS ANSWERED

About the Author

Quinita Edmonia Good is the founder and operator of Qwrites Writing & Editorial Services where she serves as writer, writing coach and editor. She was raised in Detroit, Michigan, and now lives in Bloomfield, New Jersey. She is the mother of one son and the grandmother of one beautiful grand-daughter.

Ms. Good is also an award-winning journalist. She is the recipient of two 2004 awards presented by the New Jersey Press Association, one of which is the Robert P. Kelly Newcomer of the Year Award (second place).